Yalla

FRANK S. O'NEAL

Omaha, Nebraska

© **2013 Frank S. O'Neal.** All rights reserved. No part of this publication may be reproduced in whole or in part, or stored in a retrieval system, or transmitted in any form, or by any means, electronic, mechanical, photocopying, recording, or otherwise, without written permission of the publisher. For information regarding permission, write to:

SUAD, Ltd.
2930 Parker Street
Omaha, NE 68111
www.FrankONeal.com

ISBN13: 978-0-9833885-3-1
Cataloging in Publication Data on file with publisher.

Printed in the United States of America

10   9   8   7   6   5   4   3   2

Dedication

Within the family tree are the first cousins. I am HONORED to dedicate "Yalla" to my FIRST cousins who always brought new horizons and meaning to my life.

Front Row (left to right): Bernice, Delmus, Opal
Second Row (left to right): Sandy, Mary Louise
Third Row (left to right): Ory, Earnest

Not pictured: M's Dorthy Shortridge (known as Aunt Dot), Mr. Saunder Davis (known as Cousin Sand)

At its Core

The

VALUE

Is

Our Place in RELATIONSHIPS!!!

NO Family

NO Soap…

there are Reasons

that each of US are born

Our QUEST:

To Discover Those Reasons…

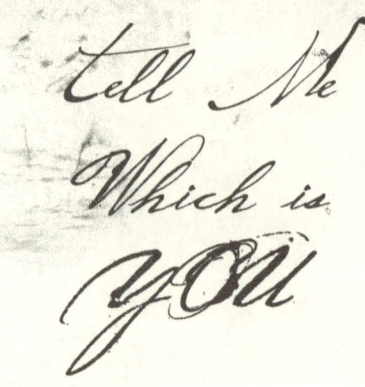
Tell Me Which is YOU

If: OUR Children are..............................OUR Future.....................

    Is it ME OR

        1 in 4 children go HUNGRY   300 Million
                                                               17 Million

    Tell Me Which is YOU

    Is it ME OR

        1 in 6 boys will fall victim to Child Abuse
                                                           Do the Math

    Tell Me Which is YOU

    Is it ME OR

        1 in 4 girls will fall victim to Child Abuse
                                                        Do the Damn Math

Tell ME

    If our Children are our Future

        PLEASE   **TELL**   **ME**

    Look what we have done to OUR Future

Any Wonder................What and Why

We have Become.................

EVER WONDER WHY

TELL ME

WHICH

IS

YOU!!!!!!

How Do We Learn

How do We Learn

        Behavior   Leadership   Love

  When you point with One
      Three point back at THEE

How do We Learn

        Law   Discipline   Diplomacy

  When you point with One
      Three point back at THEE

How do We Learn

        Passion   Compassion   Empathy

  When you point with One
      Three point back at THEE

How do We Learn the Quest for
        Knowledge   Respect   & Respectability

  When you point with One
      Three point back at THEE

Can you Clearly See

    You are ONE of the two who enjoined in Carnal, Hedonist, Self-Centered animal Sexually without thought to the consequence to the real life Reality

        The creation of the MIRACLE

        The FAMILY

    When you point with One

        Three point back at THEE

No Maturity   No Responsibility   No Quality

    To the strains of the CRETIN melodic genre

        Gotta GET that BOOTY

    When you point with One

        Three point back at THEE

YOU SEE
For it is written

"Whatever YOU do to the least of MY brethren

    YOU do unto ME,"

        When you point with One

                Three point back at THEE

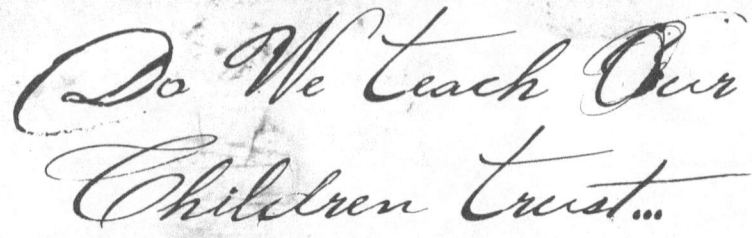

Do We Teach Our Children Trust...

Do we teach our children to TRUST

    When the parents are the abomination of BUST

Do we teach our children to TRUST

    When the parents are the primary vehicle of LUST

Do we teach our children to TRUST

    When the parents LINK to each other is prime evil sensuousness

Do we teach our children to TRUST

    When the parents encourage friendships to relieve themselves from care to US

Do we teach our children to TRUST

    When the parents encourage underage sexual FUSS

Do we teach our children to TRUST

    When the parents cannot or will NOT commit beyond ducking US

Do we teach our children to TRUST

    When the parents allow 1.5 million to go missing each year let alone CUSS

Do we teach our children to TRUST

    You pathetic SCUM. You misguided SCOURGE. You valueless Mother-ucking MESS

The TWO of YOU procreated the BEST

                            So what the duck?

Is there anybody, somebody to stand and make a FUSS?

    To teach OUR Children to TRUST!!!

What is Blackness…

        Society------------Culture
        Language----------Ethnicity

What is Society…

        Norms-------------Role
        Goal---------------Dominion

What is Culture…

        Tribal-------------Totality of Life-----In and
                                                          Of Itself to
                                                            Imfinity

What is Language…

        Means to Communicate

What is Ethnicity…

        Specialty of Each

THEREFORE: **No Family**

                                              No Soap…….

If: It's Belief that gets us There

If: Faith is the foundation of Religion

Therefore:

        Religion is as GOOD as Those

        Who espouse its' Principles'

What's

YOUR

        Story…?

The Beauty

The Beauty of Existence

                              Is LIFE

The Beauty of Life

                              Is THE Miracle

The Beauty of The Miracle

                              Is MAN

The Beauty of Man

                              Is DIVERSITY

The Beauty of Diversity

                              Is

    For All that can separate   US
    For All that is Different about   US
    Is there Anything common among   US

    Men..........................Women..........................Children

                                    Do **YOU DARE….?**

It Takes Two

In the beginning there was GOD
    GOD created MAN   IT TAKES TWO

MAN sought Dominion over Existence
    Man created Linkage to
    GOD as GOD'S messenger   IT TAKES TWO

God delivered to MAN the LAW of 10
    Man created LAW to Infamy   IT TAKES TWO

What is GOD   THEN
    What is MAN   THEN

Man decries Dominion over MAN, NATURE, & TECHNOLOGY
    Is Man then the ultimate Authority
    After ALL Man linked
    His Authority to God   IT TAKES TWO

SPIRITUAL WAY OF LIFE   MATERIAL WAY OF LIFE
         IT TAKES TWO

    Does ONE seek Dominion over the OTHER

MAN the Animal   procreates
MAN the Simpleton   emasculates
MAN the Privilege   segregates
    GOD the DIVINE MAGISTRATE incorporates   IT TAKES TWO

THEREFORE: Render to Caesar   MATERIAL
                 Render to God   SPIRITUAL

     AFTER   ALL   IT TAKES TWO

If Only......

Standing on the Bluffs overlooking MY birth vicinity
    Standing alone, NOT wanting to be alone Squinting to see
        Ultimately,
                Will YOU walk with ME
                Will YOU talk with ME
      For mistakes have COST me dearly
      "Can you FIX what's made to be broken,"
I can fix this EXCLUSIVITY…MORALLY
                ETHICALLY
                LEGALLY
                    RELIGIOUSLY

Tell me…Please tell me…
        Why does there exist these Discrepancies
Infant Mortality: Doctor PLEASE….Hypocritically----2:1
                EXCLUSIVE AMA Squeeze

Why Me…?

Educationally: State-Boards-Superintendents-AND-Federally
            50% failure Rate
            Eviscerate Culturally

Why Me…?

Religiously: Tell me BLUNTLY Ministers and Clergy…Clannishly
    "If all MEN are EQUAL under GOD,"
  Why the existence of All BLACK churches and MINISTRIES
              Calculated-Less-PURITY

Why Me…?

The Elephant…fornicatively…Still refuses to recognize, and to this
        Day challenges my Citizenry
Alas the NYMPHO Jackass enjoys only my plurality
                    YOU SEE
          "Can you FIX what's made to be broken,"
            The Eyes around me are so COLD
           With every chance They steal my soul
Emphatically……I need ANSWERS

                  I shout OUT

                      Can you hear ME

Tell Me
      Please Tell ME
          "Can you FIX what's made to be broken,"
            I CAN fix what's made to BE
Especially   This   EXCLUSIVITY
        NOT to mention SLAVERY
        NOT to mention PLESSEY

It only hurts

      It only Hurts

              It only **HURTS**

                      To **BREATHE…!!!**

If: A Jurist is seated to authoritatively adjudicate in a Court the Doctrine of EQUABLE Deliberation.

If: A Political Association is formed to PROFESS and direct Philosophical goals to be accepted by a Society through the Garnering of a PLURALITY.

If: A Jurist is a PROFESSED member of a political ASSOCIATION.

Therefore:

How is it possible or conceivable for AUTHORITATIVELY EQUABLE deliberation to OCCUR, when there exist the hyperbole of Hypocrisy BETWEEN
LETTER of the LAW   vs.   INTENT of the LAW

WHY DO YOU SMITE ME!!!

Who has the Right...

Who has the Right to take a LIFE…?
    Is It a given
        Is It a Rule of law
            Is It a Right of passage

Who has the Right to take a LIFE…?
    Is It a Right of the Divine Right of kings
        Is It a Right of a Representative form of government
        Is It Do NOT snitch

Who has the Right to take a LIFE…?

      "All POWER comes from the barrel of a GUN"
      Chairman Mao Tse Tung

Who has the RIGHT…!!!

Moral Imperative

Why did IT…
        Why did IT come to BE…
I even name my Human Species…

Why did It…
        Why did IT come to BE?
I have BUILT cities both HERE and ABROAD
I have established centers of KNOWLEDGE
              Both HERE and ABROAD
I have EXPLORED both HERE and ABROAD
I have PIONEERED both HERE and ABROAD

Why did IT……
        Why did IT come to BE?
Fruits of my LABOR . . . . God Bless Thee
Began a NATION with my UTILITY . . . . God Bless Thee
Fought a WAR for my SERVICEABILITY. . . . . God Bless Thee
The Bill of RIGHTS . . . . God Bless Thee

Why did IT…   Why did IT come to BE….

Lets SEE,
Recertification to VOTE every SIX years for ME…
                  Humanity
Adjudication for every commonplace LIBERTY of DIGNITY…
            Legitimacy

And Thus

This is DEMOCRACY…
                  Duality

Oh HELL YES   **GOD BLESS THEE**

Why did IT…………….
                Why did IT come to BE……………?

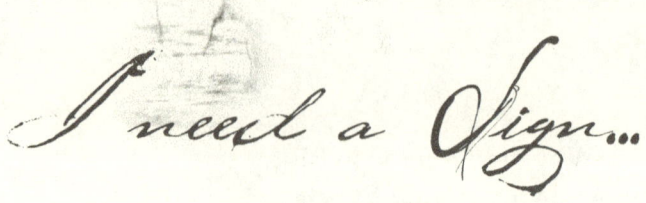

I need a Sign...

Let me know **YOU** are Here…

I need a Sign
    For I have No FEAR
    For I have My Shield and Speer
    For I have ALL My Combat Gear

I need a Sign
    Let Me know YOU are HERE

I need a Sign
    No more time to Spill My Beer
    No more time to let the Jackass and Elephant to continue to Steer
    No more time for the Divisive "535," vested PERSONAL INTEREST   Can I BE ever MORE Clear
Listen my children and YOU shall HEAR
        Value   Respect
      Honesty   Spiritually
          FAMILY

I need a Sign………………….NOW…………..

LET ME KNOW YOU ARE HERE…!!!

the House does not
rest upon the ground
but upon a woman

May I join You at Your Garden Gate......

May I join You at Your Garden GATE
    If It is only for your   Sight
    If It is only for your eyes Twinkle   Bright

May I join You at Your Garden Gate
    If It is only for your   Touch
    If It is only for your Smell….Your Taste To   Embrace

May I join You at Your Garden Gate
    If It is only to Create…That Loving Smile upon   Thy Face

May I Meet YOU
                May I Entreat YOU

May

    I

        Join YOU

            At

              YOUR GARDEN GATE…

the House does not rest upon the ground but upon a woman

May I join You at Your Garden Gate......

May I join You at Your Garden GATE
    If It is only for your   Sight
    If It is only for your eyes Twinkle   Bright

May I join You at Your Garden Gate
    If It is only for your   Touch
    If It is only for your Smell….Your Taste To   Embrace

May I join You at Your Garden Gate
    If It is only to Create…That Loving Smile upon   Thy Face

May I Meet YOU
              May I Entreat YOU

May

    I

        Join YOU

                At

YOUR GARDEN GATE…

Kiss

Is it me or just what is this

      Will of the wisp   I would be remiss

My temperature rises to this extreme abyss

My heart pounds with tremors from my ankles to my wrist

      Your Eyes penetrate to my soul without Risk

      Your Smell exacerbates the passion rush to Twist

      As you rapture Me

            As you capture Me

                And this

Compels Me

Drives Me

Encapsulate Me

            To Wish

What a Miracle

          How precious is this

              My lips to meet Yours

           For   Just

            A

        K I S S

This Bitch

Beautiful
      Intelligent
           Tenacious
      Charming
House

                    I am This Bitch
                    I'll Be This Bitch
                    So Twitch…..Witch
                              When YOU speak
                      To THIS

Beautiful and Bountiful
   Intelligent and Intellectual
      Tenacious and Tactful
         Charming and Charismatic
            House and Hit

                    Feel Me
"…Tell UR man to CLOSE his mouth 'cause he can't hit THIS"

What is the Sadness...?

What is the Sadness
      What is the Hurt
           What is the Pain
                  What is the Loneliness?
                        What is the Devastation
                              What is the Strain

What is the Emptiness
      What is the Futility
           What is the walk in the Rain
                  What is the Madness
                        What is the Consternation
                              What is the Refrain

Am I Sane?

I wonder…Stutter…and Pause… For I now have No Cause
No purpose…To Reason…
What is the Sadness   The Loneliness   The Emptiness
The Madness
I LOST the DOVE…The GLOVE…My LOVE

"'Tis better to have LOVED and LOST than NEVER LOVED at ALL"

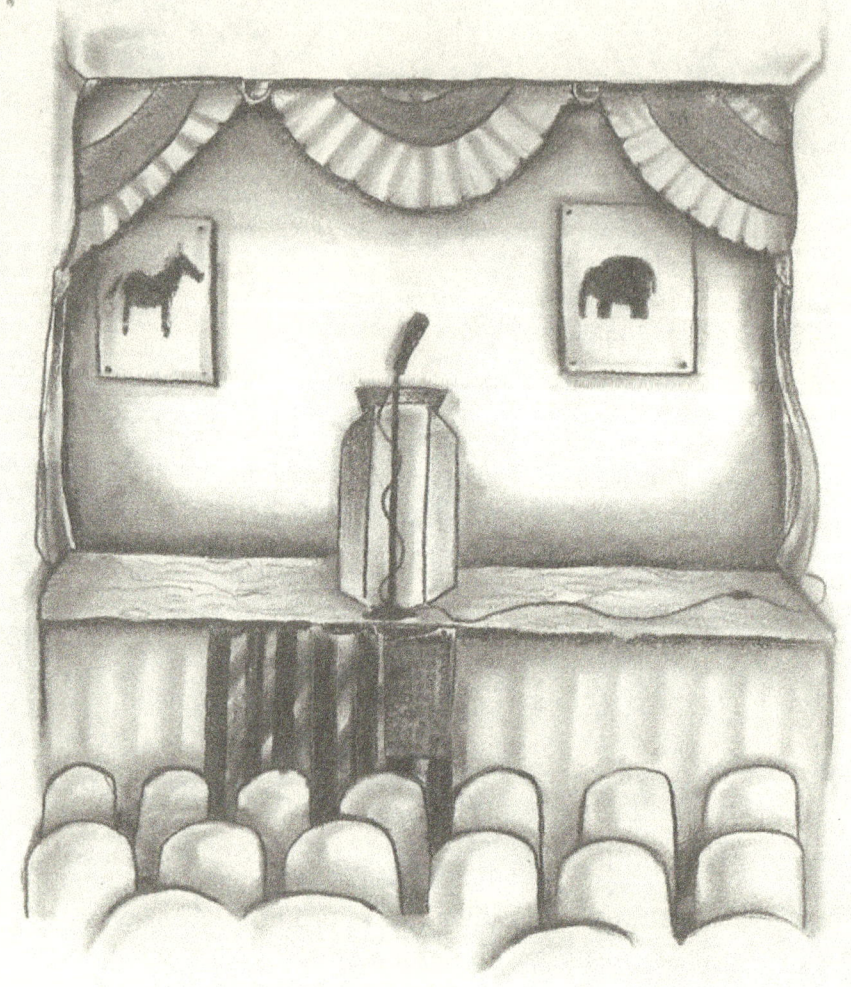

*Where were Man
Not fore
His Quest for
Order...*

the One

Have you ever dreamed OR wanted to be the ONE
Did you perceive the sacrifice,
>	The loneliness,
>>		The dedication it would take
>	To become the ONE
As I walk and gaze into this world you created…
   JUST what have I BECOME…
>	In the beginning as a child, OTHERS had to poke FUN
>	At twelve I knew that one day, in YOUR world, without
>	Inner strength I would SUCCUMB.
>	So knowledge, creativity, communication became my QUEST,
>	My inner zeal…So woe BE to YOU good buddy, when I am DONE
>	For all I ever wanted is to fit IN, have a friend, laugh, joke and party
>>		And JUST have FUN
>	But YOU always put me IN my place, to humiliate, emasculate,
>	And perpetuate that YOU are indeed the only ONE
>	I gravitate, encapsulate, and levitate YOUR pure Evil back to Hell
>	For NOW the time has COME
>	As I journey through YOUR gauntlet Valley of Death
>	With cannons to the Right… With cannons to the Left and
>	Before me, you SCUM
>	I will ride with my Sword unshielded… my Quill spewing ink
>	So I will become YOUR pest… YOUR nemesis as YOU should
>>		Remember SON

I am the ONE

To succumb
    To submit
        I will NEVER
            To be patronized
                To be chastised

        I will NEVER

To be pitied
    To be sorry for
        I will NEVER
            To be sanitized
                To be assimilated

        I will NEVER

I Query:.........?
            Human
            Legitimate
            MAN

I Never WILL!!!

If: Duty is LIVE

If: Honor is LIVE

If: Country is LIVE

What of EVIL

What of EVIL

What in the HELL
    Is of EVIL

As it is foretold… "It is always the darkest before the Dawn,"
Thou Death is the Shadow of Life…
I yearn to burn to turn ON the Light-of-Life

YO
"'Tis better to Light one candle
Than
To curse the DARKNESS"
Let
It
SHINE…!!!

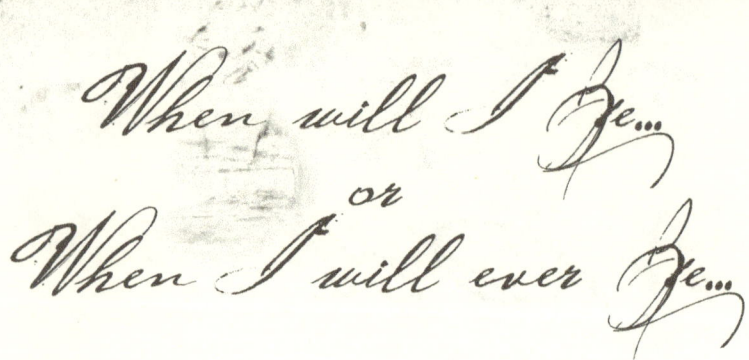

When will I Be... or When I will ever Be...

Will I ever Be
     Or Is it just ME
Chattel BE.......... Engraved Hanging TREE
Chattel BE.......... Founders needed SLAVERY
Chattel BE.......... Chattel BE .... Chattel BE

Will I ever BE
     Or Is it just ME
Chattel BE.......... Fight for me and I will set you FREE
Chattel BE.......... South to North for INDUSTRY
Chattel BE.......... Chattel BE .... Chattel BE

Will I ever Be
     Or Is it just ME.......You see......PURITY.......QUALITY....CONFORMITY
That BEs the Keys to FREE......Who Dat'......Who Dat'......Who Dat' BE
Does LIFE carry Specialty .... Or Is it just ME
Does GOD carry Exclusivity ...... Or Is it just ME
Does LAW carry Finality .... Or Is it just ME
CHATTEL BE .... NOT hardly
Jackass-Semi-BE............Too Glossy............Confounding Hypocrisy
Elephant Exclusivity............Pompous............Rigidity

Hunt Me down into the Ground, DOG

When will I BE
     Does Masser' continue his revelry

I WILL BE!!!

Capture the Dream
(Thank You Mr. Robert Griffin III)

Will YOU offer your step and stride into the Stream
    To walk the thoughts you conceived to become Supreme
    As you Rock and Roll sometimes having to duck and dodge
    Superficial Things
        The twists and turns, the moans and yearns and Love Sings
           Whoever said this would be Easy
For those who think that this would be EASY hear me Sing…
I'd could Sling, make-a-bunch-of-babies, Rob, GET that MONEY, Bling BLING
I am MORE than ROOTIN', TOOTIN', Running the streets, Shooting and always

      Running from something
I have CHOICES over running with the CROWD and always Tripping
    As a kid…When I saw my first Plane Flying….
      I am Good ENOUGH
I am and will be Smart ENOUGH wading through the Journey of Life Stream
      TO VALUE and Even MORE
        Capture the Dream

"I BELIEVE I CAN FLY…….."

Can WE with OUR empirical and knowledge Based System

Systematically
Via
Cultural Arrogance

Prove the validity of the DEPRAVITY of MAN

Bite the HAND that feeds US

Become GOD

"A sad SOUL can KILL you quicker….QUICKER Than a GERM"……….John Steinbeck

Double

(Poem one travels to Poem Two)

While it is Cloudy overhead
                Does this Preclude Streams of Sunny & Bright
As I sit and ponder the yonder
      IT has Rained Today
           Is SHE nourishing…All of Us…OR…Some of Us
Through the fonder reflections of Family and History
In this small faint visual mystery
      IT has Rained Today
           Will SHE honor…All of Us…OR…Some of Us
Beset on this bench surrounded in Rich Symmetry
      It has Rained Today
           Is SHE preventing…All of Us…OR…Some of Us
In times less hectic without Wizardry
BLESSED Peace and unadulterated Harmony
      It has Rained Today
           Will SHE nourish, Will SHE honor, Will SHE Prevent
           All of Us…Or…Some of Us
Chirp, Chirp from the Left…A Robin's lullaby…A Gentle Breeze………
      It has Rained Today
           Am I one of All of Us…OR…Some of Us
While time forever standing still to chill the Quill and curse the still is No Thrill
      Pray tell who is this US
      Pray tell who are All of US
      Pray tell who are some of US
Encapsulate ME to BE one with Thee
      Et.al. Drop-Dead-Gorgeous-Populous

It has Rained Today

(The New & Improved ...u ...x ...n)

You know these Men   You know Them Well
        Holders of PURITY
        Holders of JUSTICE
        Holders of HONESTY
        Holders of RIGHTEOUSNESS

Yes my friends, holders of American LIBERTY
    Where do THEY come from
        Who do THEY be
            Holders of My LIBERTY……NOT HARDLY!!!

Animals-----------Procreate

Simpletons--------Emasculate

The Privileged----Segregate

I will NOT speculate as to their Innate dominant ability to Segregate, Disassociate, Procrastinate, Masturbate, and Emasculate every of color Primate, as well as, Formulate, Manipulate, Exasperate, and Postulate, to Ingratiate to their Novitiate THEIR Divine Right to Magistrate and Legislate   THEY will always be better than WE the People..............

Oh Say can YOU SEE   **The Tea Party…!!!**

(Thank You Rex)

To Implore the Quest is to SEEK
To Seek the Implore is to EXPLORE
To Explore the Seek is to EXAMINE
To Examine the Explore is to CLARIFY
To Clarify the Examine is to EMBODY
To Embody the Clarify is to ENGAGE
To Engage the Embody is to EMBRACE
To Embrace the Engage is to VALUE
To Value the Embrace is to LOVE

        To SEEK

EXPLORE		EXAMINE
CLARIFY	EMBODY	ENGAGE
EMBRACE	VALUE	LOVE

HUMANITY

Acknowledgments

To all who view, Greetings and Salutations?

I would like to express the greatest gift of all... and that is when you come in contact with other human beings you give and receive the honor and respect due. However there are times when people go out of their way to contribute, and for me, these people have made my dream come true!

Camille Steed
Lifelong friend since childhood. By her efforts I would have NEVER met Neville and Michelle. And just like when we were kids, always injected her wise vision.

Felicia Webster,
The First Lady of Spoken Word-in-Omaha
Whenever I needed advice, she was there, and assisted me greatly with my delivery through her performance.

Daniel Nicol,
Illustrator Volume III *Yalla*
I could see in your eyes that you could "see" my vision. Thank you for lending your skilled hand to the visual adapation of my words.

Concierge Marketing, Inc.
Genius is a delicacy desired by all. Some may flirt with it, some may take a shot in the dark, some find it by accident, and some nibble around the edges. Concierge Marketing is genius personified from Lisa at the top to Alison, Jessica and Ellie—pure integrity. For without you, where would I be? Je Temme.

It has always been said to save the BEST for last:
So therefore it is my HONOR, my privilege, and my pleasure to honor the entire staff of Metro Community College-South Campus.

Especially the Dean of Students, the Business College et al. teachers and staff, and more importantly the individual teachers all of whom have taken the time to give me consul, advice, and helpful hints to make my journey and dreams come true.

www.ingramcontent.com/pod-product-compliance
Lightning Source LLC
Chambersburg PA
CBHW051720040426
42446CB00008B/972